Edition Schott

arren-Archiv

Leo Brouwer
*1939

3 Apuntes
3 Sketches
3 Skizzen

para Guitarra
for Guitar
für Gitarre

GA 426
ISMN 979-0-001-09676-8

www.schott-music.com

Mainz · London · Berlin · Madrid · New York · Paris · Prague · Tokyo · Toronto

TRES APUNTES

Three Sketches / Drei Skizzen

I - De el „Homenaje a Falla"

from „Homenaje a Falla" / aus „Homenaje a Falla"

Leo Brouwer
(1959)

Poco meno (quasi Andantino)
legato liberamente
accel.
Tempo I
più stacc.
poco
cresc. molto
cresc.
pizz.
nat.
(metálico)

II - De unfragmento instrumental

From a chamber music piece / Aus einem Kammermusikwerk

III- Sobre un canto de Bulgaria

On a Bulgarien Song / Über ein bulgarisches Lied

*) "apoyando" ind. y anular. (i., a.) / *) "Supported stroke" (i., a.) / *) Anschlag mit Anlegen (i., a.)

C3
¢2
dim.sempre
poco
dim.
rall.
sosten.
molto rall.
ARM. 12
p